TOP LEGITIMATE

PASSIVE INCOME JOBS

By Daniel Udom

Copyright© April, 2019 by Daniel Udom

No part of this publication may be reproduced or transmitted in any form or by any means, electronic or mechanical, including photocopying, recording, or by any information storage or retrieval system, without permission in writing from the publisher.

All publishing rights belong exclusively to:
DANUDS ONLINE VENTURES,
3, Stadium Lane, Etinan,
Akwa Ibom State,
NG.

FOREWORD

Passive Income Jobs

What is a passive income business? It is no big secret. Passive income has to do with the capability to earn money, doing simple things, without direct, every day involvement in the process. If there is one thing you should understand, it is that absolutely everyone could build a passive income online business, given the tools and the determination. Then you are knowledgeable about the concept, if you've ever known anybody who owned a property. A person who rents out it and buys an apartment does not need to put in 10 hours every day to have a return. They could unwind and allow the money roll in once they've done the work of fixing it up, purchasing, and renting it out. Sure, there could be a few day care that is small, but the work was done.

You have heard about making strategies and venturing into new fields of endeavor, but you probably dismissed them for people who've a promotion or web creation background as scams or something. You need to modify your way of thinking and come to this understanding that you can be an entrepreneur, if you want to quit working 50 or 60 hours per week for a business which can reposition you for a big deal within a few hours of work.

This is the definition of income that is passive. It is easier to begin an online enterprise. Among the best ways to do it is through internet affiliate marketing. You may get into affiliate internet marketing in just one of two ways. One, you might utilize it as a tool. Let us say you wrote an eBook or designed an on-line game. How do you get individuals to buy your product? Affiliate internet marketing does the work for you. You just let others do all your promotion in exchange for a piece of the sales price. You do not need to do a thing, which is the epitome of passive income.

Standard income doesn't eliminate the desire or possibility for individuals to earn money by working, it merely means that you don't have to think about starving or getting evicted as you do it. Passive income is normally defined as a stream of income earned with little if any continuing effort needed from the person receiving the passive income to be able to grow the stream of revenue.

You may also get into affiliate internet marketing from the other side. You may be an affiliate and begin your passive income enterprise that way. Find a merchandise you believe in and become an affiliate. Go out and advertise that merchandise in all the ways you can. Once you have built an internet site or blog, or purchased advertisements, you won't have to do much more. It is not as if you have to go knocking on doors or make cold calls. A passive income enterprise is among the only ways you could make more money while working less.

The Author

CONTENT	Page
Copyright	ii
Foreword	iii
Content	v
1. BENEFITS OF PASSIVE INCOME JOBS	1
2. LEGITIMATE WORK AT HOME ONLINE JOBS	4
3. TOP LEGIT ONLINE JOBS SECRET	11
4. BLOGGING	14
5. AFFILIATE INTERNET MARKETING	17
6. ARTICLE MARKETING	20
7. PAY-PER-CLICK ADVERTISING	23
8. FREELANCING JOBS	26
9. DATA ENTRY JOBS	29
10. KINDLE DIRECT PUBLISHING	32
11. EMAIL MARKETING	35
12 HOW TO BECOME AN AMAZON ASSOCIATE	38
13. BULK SMS TEXT MESSAGING	41
14. DEVELOPING MOBILE APPLICATIONS	45
15. SOCIALMEDIA MARKETING	48
16. FACEBOOK MARKETING	50

17. PARTICIPATION IN USABILITY TESTING OF APPS	54
18. REGISTRATION ON REWARD SITES	57
19. DOCUMENT TRANSLATION	59
20. JOINING SURVEY PANELS	63
21. HOW TO EARN FROM HUBPAGES	66
22. REAL ESTATE INVESTMENT	69
23. DROPSHIPPING	71
24. EARNING FROM MYSPACE ACCOUNT	79
25. MAKING MONEY FROM EBAY	85
26. MY RECOMMENDATIONS	90

1. BENEFITS OF PASSIVE INCOME JOBS

Residual income or passive income is something which is earned by men and women who own a part-time internet enterprise. Earning passive income ought to be the aim of every individual in the long-run.

Additional income can be generated for the exact same quantity of time worked, and one must still work for a time for it. Passive income doesn't signify that it is possible to earn money without working. Rather, it is a powerful tool in one's financial strategy that one earns more while he works less, leveraging a little input to gain a great output! There are some key concepts that you should understand so you can plan effectively.

An income that is passive might be attained whenever you are generating income without directly getting involved in the challenging work. You cannot generate passive income if you do not know how to systematically go about it, which is just why most individuals do not earn any automated income. The residual income is the ideal approach to discover a source to create money automatically to find income monthly with no type of disturbances in it. In order to get a good amount of residual income every month one should have self determination and be patient. So then you simply can raise your earnings.

If you are lucky enough you may find some home based work that you fully enjoy. Imagine that, you compete with different folks very hard and receive a work eventually but that job isn't a job which you like in any respect. Jobs have to be found and competed with others. If you opt to work in a business, you must compete with others to find the job. You are able to quit working and your income stream still does the job constantly. Because with passive income, you can get multiple streams of income, thus you may also be more secure financially. You might have as many diverse streams of income as you want. This would build into a company.

After the company is ready to go, it is going to generate income for you even when you do not spend an excessive amount of time on it. Actually, many are scared to grow their businesses in any respect, because they believe it will mean more work and more stress. By comparison, passive revenue business is not necessarily to be on the work every minute, every hour, everyday. Because once you've got your passive revenue business going, you'll be making a huge sum of cash with little effort. Should you run your very own passive revenue company, you can get the job done alone without other folks. For your very own passive income company, you'll do your very best.

You've got to compete with others to acquire promotion prospects. Finding the proper passive revenue opportunity can require some research, but the majority of people believe it to be well worth the effort. You are able to take advantage of their services to earn some additional income. For example, you can take advantage of a program such as the Google AdSense if you wish to understand how to earn money without stress.

There are different ways that you could make money in an instantaneous way. Most people have a tendency to save all of the money they earn after taking out the monthly expenses. The cash you earn without spending much time is what is described as passive income.

There are a number of ways to earn money from real estate market. Even if you decide to begin making some money, it might not be sufficient to support you and your loved ones. Generate money from those tasks you're doing. Yes, you can definitely generate some money when doing some things you are used to. An individual can raise a fortune just spending money on the correct place. It is simpler to earn money here in case you have a good amount of money to make investments. It is possible to earn more cash by giving more efforts to increase you passive income thus you could be able to save more money without sacrificing your present lifestyle. Some individuals even make more cash from their website than their stressful company jobs!

2. **<u>LEGITIMATE WORK AT HOME ONLINE JOBS</u>**

Legitimate work at home. This is beautiful! It is great! Its beauty lies in its flexibility. You can be working in a relaxed condition, working under a shade tree, working in your bed room, staying at the sea shore at even at the back of a commuter in a busy town. What matters where? In as much as you have you internet connectivity, your laptop or your smart phone, you are good to go.

If you wish to develop your own home based business then you should be ready for some challenges. Prove you could do the job effectively from home. Usually, it's simple to decide you want to earn from home. Well, it is the very same with working at home. There are enough home based work opportunities readily available online by which an individual can fix all types of financial issues. There are several legal sites which provide facility of exploring internet home enterprise. An additional way it's possible to find work on the internet is to look for companies who require work completed for them. You won't have the ability to begin earning money on the internet in case you don't take action. There are usually two primary methods to generate money on the internet. The only real method to make money on the internet is to become educated and produce the skills which you will need to develop into successful program. There are real methods of earning money online, and in addition, there are the not so real ways. If a program is capable to solve some life problems, then it serve the purpose, because people will certainly look for you and your services.

With the state of the economy, it's important to locate legitimate work from home that will offer you the security and flexibility to make your company a success. A legitimate work at home opportunity is simple to spot. Legitimate home based jobs are going to have legitimate physical address not merely a P.O.Box and will also maintain a permanent site. For such individuals, legitimate work at home jobs can be found on the Internet where companies post their requirements on the web and obtain their work done from freelancers. In that case, it will seem attractive if you have some unfulfilled dreams that you want to fulfill. There are however several great legitimate works at home jobs, if you know the best place to look, if you be sure that you look at the BBB for the company, and should you make certain to check other referral and rating websites, as a way to be certain that the business you are handling is truly legit. On the exact same token, in addition, there are many very legitimate work at home jobs and ones in which you are able to make a significant steady income.

If you become aware of, not all of these have a normal job. As already pointed out, the micro jobs being offered are simple to do and can be done in a quick timeframe. A remote job is only a job which isn't performed in an office. The legitimate jobs exist and there are many stay at home moms which are truly benefiting from everything they have to give. If you're looking for internet data entry jobs, there are a few real options out there. Data entry jobs and writing tasks are some of the common on-line jobs.

One of the excellent advantages of working on the internet is that all you've got to have is a computer and an online connection. The chance to work at home is great. If your opportunity ticks off all of the above boxes, then there's a good probability that you are in possession of a viable and lucrative long-term business on your hands. It's too simple and good of a chance for people not to look at trying out. There are quite a lot of opportunities for men and women that are seeking to work at home online.

While there are tons of work at home scams on the web; yet, in addition, there are legitimate opportunities. Finding legit work at home can be difficult if you don't experience a comprehension of the markers that help determine whether a particular business represents a very good risk. Therefore, if you'd like to go for legit home based alternatives, then you have to take a look on Internet first. If you're devoted to finding a job it can definitely be done, though it is going to take a good deal of motivation and determination. In the event you figure out what that can be done, home business online jobs might be the ideal option for everyone who wishes to take more time in your home. In the majority of instances, it's not really the specific at home work for moms that you're choosing but rather, it's your perspective of that work. There are numerous home based ideas out there that you could do.

Showing you how ANYONE can earn money online working at home.

Making money online simply is not that easy or many others would do it. Therefore, if you want to earn some cash online and be in a position to work at home, then here are a couple of ways to do precisely that.

Your site ought to be attractive, user-friendly, and simple to navigate. You will be, taken to a site that offers you all of the info that you will need to start generating your great income with legit online jobs at the moment. It is hard to discover websites offering an excellent service free of charge. It's actually essential that you have your own site, and when you don't you won't be in a position to properly target the appropriate audience. It's rather easy to develope your own site if you make the most of many free learning opportunities online.

Another solution to avoid being conned is to look for internet sites that are paid or at least take time to inquire into the site if it's credible and dependable.

If you wish to make a good sum of money on a normal basis, make sure that you register with dozens of survey sites. Whichever job you're planning to undertake to earn money, there are a couple salient things which you want to think about essentially. You could start earning money as little as a couple of days. After submitting a small quantity of ads, you can begin seeing money appear in your on-line bank account. If you want to earn some actual money online, then you should check out article advertising. You're promised with higher pay for little work.

In starting a company, you do have to work hard in order to be successful. If you search by business type you will have to know the kind of business you are searching for. The internet businesses deliver such stipulations of working. Considering all the competition in pay-per-click advertising, it is problematic for a small business to come on top of the search engines. There are lots of home-based businesses which are associated with Internet.

Internet affiliate marketing is a superb means to earn some additional money from home but it does take work. Online affiliate marketing is in my opinion one of the simplest methods to earn money from home provided that you're prepared to do some work, however it is advisable to do your research rather than just signing up with the very first business you see. On-line advertising has skyrocketed over the last few years. Article marketing will permit you to earn money online now by creating a commission from your sales.

There are a number of online jobs out there and legitimate platforms where you are able to see them. Online writing jobs are growing increasingly more each day because of a demand for original articles. Legitimate on-line jobs won't ever charge a fee. With just a little diligence and some excess effort on your part, you'll have the ability to land at a legitimate on-line job immediately! Legit on-line job is quite available! Possibly among the most effective legit on-line jobs and among the greatest legit on-line job sites is the one which describes how people throughout the world can get the job done for the significant businesses.

Explore the many advantages of jobs online. Online jobs basically are jobs you can do from the comfort of your house. Any time that you're seeking an on-line job for stay at home dads it is necessary to remember the time you've got available, your abilities and the passion you've got to put forth the effort needed to keep up your position, whether you're freelancing or if you wish to work from home for many years to come.

One other point to be on the watch for while seeking work at home jobs is there are lots of people out there publishing online job opportunities that are only scams. Because you won't have an immediate contact legit work at home jobs and also be really challenging to judge an individual only utilizing the details given by him. Finding the nanny jobs isn't invariably an effortless job but it is one which is so powerful. For example, if you feel your work is getting monotonous you've got the choice to change over to some other job. There are many work at home companies out there seeking to employ folks to work from home each and every day.

Explore the many advantages of jobs online.

Online jobs basically are jobs you could do from the comfort of your house. On-line data entry jobs have plenty of hype around them. They are simply mechanical jobs in nature.

You choose what sort of job that you need to perform for five dollars or more and post it to the site. With a bit of diligence and some extra effort on your part, you'll have the ability to land a legitimate on-line job very quickly! Become an Online Expert. One of the simplest online jobs you are able to get is to offer coaching assistance to someone, that is if you've already been trained at the school. One other great thing about legit online jobs is the fact by the methods they're teaching you. Any sort of legit on-line job is available! There are several legit on-line jobs and opportunities, everyday more people use the internet so as to locate their dream online job or the information which they require. There are various sorts of home based online jobs around. There are a great deal of approaches to monetize work at home online jobs.

Most legit work at home jobs require a certain kind of skills as is true with the majority of jobs on the market too.

At this time you will find jobs from home. Not to mention, you will probably make more cash doing jobs from home rather than out of your house. It is now the finest and the simplest approach to come across jobs from home.

Finding the correct job

. Legit on-line Job is essentially a membership website. Such jobs do not demand higher education qualification in addition to being carried out easily. On the flip side, if you wish to abide by a more stable day job at the office, well, it is still possible to make good use of the web.

3. **TOP LEGIT ONLINE JOBS SECRET**

The Internet is simply there, and the ideal jobs might just be two or three clicks away. It has made it possible for anyone and everyone to enjoy a nice, stable income from home. Everyday folks are turning to the web to earn money online now. Working online can assist you in many ways. Therefore, if you're looking to earn some cash online and be in a position to work at home, then here are a couple of ways to do precisely that. Making money online actually is easy once you adhere to a single course, respond, and prevent becoming sidetracked. Everyone I know is trying popular methods to earn money on the internet by utilizing all sorts of money making methods.

The intent and purport of the on-line survey companies are to help the corporate clientele with different small business backgrounds in conducting a survey about them on a particular subject. Unfortunately, it may be time-consuming to acquire employment on the website since the better part of the employers tend to be quite picky and you wind up redoing your work lots of times though you believe you did it well but overall, it is a legitimate place to find employment. Legitimate on-line work is in reality a program
on the internet which will provide you in-depth and exclusive connections with companies and thoroughly profitable individuals and will have you advertise for their company. Finding an internet job for stay at home dads can be accomplished with persistence and a comprehension of how to start landing new prospective customers and customers for the position you've envisioned for yourself. A web-based recruitment tool would be a terrific long-term investment for virtually any organization.

With legitimate on-line jobs you are able to discover an opportunity that will pay total time consistently even on autopilot! Where is it possible to locate a business opportunity that provides a network like that. On-line opportunities offer flexibility. Yet another significant issue is the fact that it's more suitable to get into job opportunities which are preferably of somebody's preference and not only copying others. You are able to either search for job opportunities which have been posted or apply and await an employer to give you an interview. An authentic on-line opportunity will provide step-by-step videos and tutorials and explain just what you will be doing for them. There are lots of opportunities for a number of skills and talents.

advantage of online courses is just the flexible schedule. There are many opportunities for folks to start straight away. Luckily, there are employment opportunities in the on-line fraternity that are legitimate. Having confidence in your abilities and what you need to offer is not just a means to discover new opportunities for revenue online, but it is likewise essential when you wish to appeal to hiring managers and prospective employers that have a vested interest in you.

4. BLOGGING

Blogging is a means to demonstrate your side for a writer.

Blogging is fantastic fun, and it may also be very profitable. Blogging is likely to make you to find out more about your passion. Blogging has gotten more popular than ever. Blogging is among the commonest methods of on-line content and may be used for all stages of Inbound marketing. Blogging for Creative Entrepreneurs is made to help you succeed by making the majority of your on-line advertising strategy.

Starting a blog can be somewhat daunting. A blog may be used to help others. A blog can be started just as a pastime or maybe to give information to family members and friends. Finally, your blog ought to have a theme, an objective. A blog that's about YOU is really hard to monetize. You can also produce a blog on your site utilizing top-level domain name.

Many people continue to be confused as to the reason why folks post blogs. Your blog ought to be something which inspires you since you know that even if things aren't rosy now, with time people will begin to look closely at your message. Your blog should have content that is interesting for people to read. They provide an insight into the lives of so many people. If you would like to create a completely free blog, you can log on to any of the sites that offer completely free blogs.

Your blog is not yet been known since it's still new. The kind of blog you maintain will also determine what sort of audience you've got.

The more focused a blog is, the more quickly you will earn with this. There are lots of ways for a blog to add potential to your site. Based on how you decide on a blog up, you ought to start making money with a blog in a couple of weeks. A blog cannot only be used for marketing, but in addition, a home-based business or a personal opinionated platform.

Sometimes it looks like everybody has a blog. To begin with, let's break down the term blog.

Making money with blogs is reasonably easy, as long as you begin out by planning before you produce your blog.

If you simply need a blog to share with your buddies, relatives, co-workers, etc. then it isn't important. If you would like to begin a blog, WordPress is possibly the simplest and most user friendly application you may use. Possessing a blog on the exact same domain will increase the quantity of pages which are part of your site.

Essentially, a blog is similar to your own personal diary. Blogs, and academic blogging specifically, have been in existence for quite a long time. If you own a blog, you've got to write blog posts! It is possible to also apply your blog to advertise an item, and to drive visitors to your site, but others haven't any site and use their blog as their sole communications window on the world wide web.

5 AFFILIATE INTERNET MARKETING

Affiliate internet marketing is a means for start-up entrepreneurs to make extra money without the true need to stock on tangible products which are being sold. It is absolutely crucial for online success and can be profitable with the right approach. Affiliate internet promotion is one of the very best and simplest methods to earn money online, but even better in case the customer is added to your email list before being sent to download their buy. You see, affiliate internet marketing allows you to work from practically anywhere you opt for, live anywhere you wish to on the planet, providing they have an online connection, and make a fantastic income at the very same time.

It has become more popular in recent years and affiliate internet marketing is among the most popular. If you search for affiliate internet marketing on an internet search engine, you can find multiple million websites offering some sort of affiliate internet products or some sort of means to publicize your website. Go here and join for a fantastic offer.

However much marketing that you want to do, you can't need to spend a lot to do it and now it's time to get to do the job. Affiliate Internet Marketing is among those categories of home business that are generating waves.

It is another way that you can make money by selling other people's product.

As soon as you have applied and been approved for your affiliate programs you will want to prepare your distinctive affiliate url's. Affiliate programs are located everywhere on the web. A fantastic affiliate program will supply you with huge commissions as well as time. Particularly if your affiliate program is offering a great sale. If you anticipate joining an online marketing affiliate program, make certain that you sign up for programs that provide you the absolute most advantage.

Recommendations

If you join an online advertising affiliate program it's great to have your own blog.

You're usually provided affiliate tools to market the goods, which makes it very simple to promote. To me affiliate tools are extremely important, and the total product. Some affiliate advertising tips include learning how to use affiliate advertising tools, and being in a position to choose what affiliate programs are reliable and will earn you the most money. Another of the affiliate online marketing tips is to have the ability to find a trustworthy affiliate program that will earn you money.To make sure your affiliate advertising success, the most crucial issue is to never stop trying. One of the absolute most powerful internet advertising strategies is to create a loyal customer base. An Internet company is equally as easy as it sounds. Although most businesses can create an excellent item, not every company is skilled in marketing. Everyone can learn to build a thriving on-line business, but making money on the web isn't a get rich quick scheme. In two or three months your company should begin to look nice and profitable. Among the advantages which you will enjoy from affiliate advertising business are you become your own boss, which means nobody will dictate for you when and what things to do.

The internet web site affiliate program promotion is presently among the best ways to make good income online.

An Affiliate (also called a Publisher)

Becoming affiliates or internet advertising resellers isn't tricky. Thus, you're prepared to turn into an affiliate marketer. An affiliate who is well established as an online marketer and has a following is a good asset to any online marketer, however big he is. Internet marketers are aware that a very good affiliate is quite valuable and they take care of those. The ideal way to learn to develop into a strong online marketer is to venture out and to let yourself learn from your own mistakes.

6 ARTICLE MARKETING

Lots of people become discouraged and even quit at article marketing only because they do not get results straight away. It Expands your success with your article by posting it on social media sites. It provides you free traffic and you want to be able to get much of that traffic to your website. Before you use article marketing, there are some things you must keep in mind. Article promotion is one of the numerous site promotion tools available. Bum marketing, also referred to as article marketing is a way of promoting a web site free of charge.

Article marketing is a rather strong means of generating traffic and reputation for your affiliate advertising enterprise. It doesn't require a large amount of money to market your product or service. It can seem like a scary prospect for an amateur of internet marketing. It is not only a way to promote a product without a website, it has massive SEO impact if you do have a website. It is a very powerful campaign, one that should not be taken lightly.

For each product that you want to promote with article marketing, attempt to write 30 articles utilizing relevant key terms. In reality you're able to start article marketing free of charge, so long as you possess some skill in writing. Unlike banners and classified ads, article marketing provides this kind of in-depth description of a solution or service which the reader is going to be prompted to see your internet website. It is an internet business model that is used mostly by online companies to promote and sell many types of products and items. It is an extraordinary tool to enhance your internet marketing efforts. Make certain that you're always trying to find out more about methods like article marketing if you want to make an impact in the industry world.

Report Marketing is one of my favorite procedures of building my network advertising enterprise. As stated before, it is one of the simplest and fastest ways for businesses to attract new customers. It is one of the good tools to improve ranking of your website. It is one of the most recommended strategies to promote your own website online. Article marketing, if developed from the newest needs of the viewers, can increase the on-line traffic of that website.

You can't write one article per week and expect it to have any actual effect on your business enterprise, or your bottom line. So if you're likely to use articles to advertise your site or a solution or both, have pride and write it yourself. Articles are a distinctive and strong type of content to utilize in lots of ways. There are some, who think you need to only submit your articles to a couple of the very best article directories. If you make articles that individuals may wish to read, you are going to have good head start. Whether you're writing articles for your affiliate advertising site, blog or maybe to submit to other websites, your article is only going to attract attention if your headline is worded properly.

To have your article read

Ideally, you would like your articles to end up ranked for some kind of search on Google. On the flip side, articles can speak about a few issues in a deeper way. Creating articles for marketing success is comparatively simple to achieve if you're

consistent and have the patience to construct on that which we know about online marketing.

Your articles ought to be wanting to educate your readers. It is very clear that articles are simple to produce and pretty straightforward. Every written article corresponds to the sort of life coach business you're in.

Everyone can churn out $1 articles, but it doesn't indicate the quality will be good. You should be aware that articles are the primary focus of article advertising. The keyword-focused articles ought to be posted to internet directories with a substantial readership.

7   **PAY- PER – CLICK ADVERTISING**

Do a comprehensive job of researching any advertising method you mean to use. In order to maintain a business running fully, it is a necessity. Ultimately, PPC advertising may be a bit unstable due to the uprising competition of different websites.

Advertising is about minimum words equals to maximum effect. Then pay per click might not be feasible for small businesses. Paid advertising would end up being a costly affair for you, in the event you don't understand how to earn ad groups, research keywords and run ad campaigns.

Advertising is about minimim words results to maximum effects. It is a common advertising method used by webmaster and business owners who want to strengthen their online presence.

Search engines are flooded with a lot of ads. So rather than hiring people to publicize your business on the opposite side of the nation, you can merely make your ads visible to the internet users in that area with merely a couple of clicks. It is essential that you're in a position to recognize which ads are earning great benefits and which aren't.

You decide whenever your ads appear. Ads ought to be directly connected to the principal web page. You are then going to be in a position to move the ad into rotation with different ads that have similar search phrases. Don't forget that the purpose is NOT to get people to click your ads, but to make sales. Drop ads that aren't performing well for you and concentrate on the ones which are.

For your campaigns to accomplish a higher Quality Score, it is necessary for you to optimize your ads with the help of these pieces of advice. PPC campaigns ensure your advertising and marketing dollars go so far as feasible offer immediate outcomes. It is an essential tool for every successful online business. PPC campaigns have become increasingly more important in establishing a superb online presence for virtually any business which takes their marketing seriously.

Flexibility

PPC campaigns also permit a degree of flexibility that is simply not feasible with other marketing and advertising practices.

PPC is really not a sensible decision for small business owners. Though PPC has many advantages, there are lots of risks connected with its efforts. PPC even gives you the ability to decide the times of the day as soon as your ads are most active. Pay Per Click (PPC) Advertising is among the absolute most efficient and productive kinds of advertising on the web.

Its hard work, but you are aware that the men and women you attract are suitable for your organization. If you are beginning a new business, it's a significant place to initiate with. If you've got an on-line business then through pay per click you can foster your small business.

On the other hand, it will help you rank quickly on top pages.

Your site is your internet store. When you're learning how to earn a site, you'll want to come across various alternatives to find the traffic needed and to construct your ranking when getting noticed by direct traffic. Your site is the face of your organization, therefore it needs to appear good. For a completely new site, it's even more important.

You don't need to spend money on the website till you get direct visitors to your website. Your site is precisely the same way. Just making an excellent website can't serve your purpose but in case you will earn a well-optimized site, you are definitely going to earn excellent returns.

8 FREE – LANCING JOBS

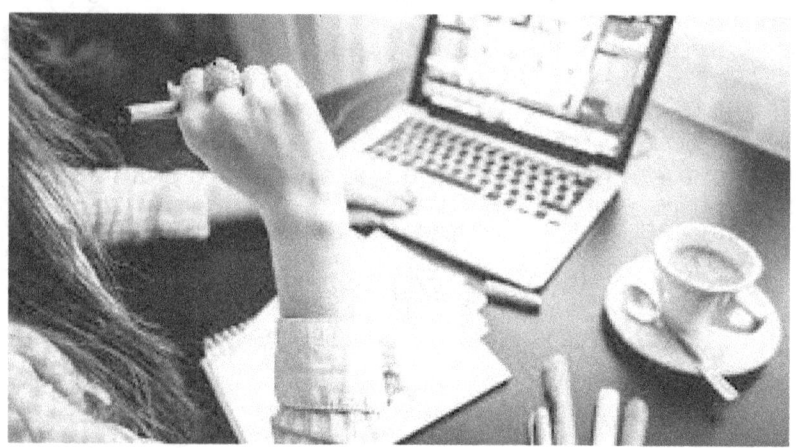

Apply by telling how much experience you've got and the way you want to complete the job. You must be very self-motivated and ready to get on with the job of generating business, despite the fact that you might not always feel like it. In most instances the jobs are odd. The most frequent method of requesting a conventional job is composing a cover letter that shows how you're qualified. You'll see lots of low-budget jobs on here, but you can also locate terrific clients who are eager to pay well. There's probably a completely free lancing job readily available in every area.

You can do freelancing on virtually any kind of work you can imagine. Whatever you can do, do it well. Put a Master's touch to it, you can stand out with dexterity and earn from it. A fortunate one may receive a job. If you're a fantastic writer, you can acquire freelance jobs for writing. Home based freelance jobs are offered for individuals who are ready to do it. It's unlikely you'll want to keep sending out resumes and searching for work, which is frequently the custom of freelancers who are attempting to establish their client base. You'll most likely be in a position to earn more in case you offer the proper type of services to the ideal clients. Offer the most suitable service to the appropriate customers, packaged in the ideal way, and your market value goes way up. At the

end of a week, the customer chooses the ideal design, and that designer becomes paid. Small business users can post work or search freelancer profiles.

If you may pass, they're a fantastic organization to acquire in with.

For any sort of business to be successful, you've got to go paid. If your small business wants a consultant to control an important small business undertaking, then SkillBridgeis the place to search. It can find a journalist to write articles using PitchMe.org. Everyone ought to be thinking about developing a business," says Barrie. With the growth of e-commerce and internet shopping, affiliate marketing has also risen as an excellent supply of making money from home.

Besides a more flexible work schedule, freelancers are generally happy. Freelancers seeking to make extra money can become "Taskers". One of the primary differences in obtaining a conventional job versus a freelance writing job is that almost all people today expect the conventional job to last a little while. Rather than being in a rush to take your purchase, our professionals slow down and take the opportunity to educate you on that which we feel will get the job done best.

Experience isn't essential as full training will be supplied. When you get started freelancing, the experience that you gain from it may be used to acquire higher paying projects later on. You require basic small business abilities. You are able to find talent for nearly any knowledge industry speciality your business may need. If you would like to create a huge team in a small quantity of time then the Upwork team can assist you with their distinctive enterprise services.

9 **DATA ENTRY JOBS**

Data entry requires very little specific training, therefore it's fairly simple to get started. It is the process of converting process data from one form to another form. It is a simple job that does not need any technical knowledge. Since it usually only requires a computer and a keyboard, clerks often find that they can work from home. It is one of the simplest jobs that are available online that you are able to do to work from home and earn money. It seems to go hand in hand with spreadsheet work 75% of the time. Data entry posting jobs are offered all around the net, but it is a fantastic concept to be selective when selecting fantastic company.

When you locate a job, you may apply via contact provide. Most jobs do need a simple high school education or GED. It is possible to hardly see that you are improving if you simply concentrate on your work. One other important point to consider is you should fully understand the job which you're doing and you have to be proficient enough to understand and follow instructions from clients and employers carefully. Home data entry jobs provide great flexibility, not to mention you've already taken that under consideration, but there are a couple of different things that you should prepare for to avoid being taken by surprise early in the work change.

As soon as your occupation is approved, you're going to be paid in the check amount. Then the data entry job is offered in any provider promptly. Having data entry jobs from home may require that you have specific skills that you should enhance.

You've got to outsource the job in order not to compromise the organization in any job which will not be completed. There are different kinds of jobs out there in the internet market. You can do the work even from the comforts of your house. As an issue of fact, a lot of people have quit their regular 9-5 jobs to concentrate on various data entry jobs which they could do at home. Home-based freelance jobs are offered for individuals who are ready to do it. Many professional jobs utilize a kind of information entry. A stable full-time remote job is a clear possibility.

If you're looking for a job which you should have a resume. Data entry jobs have come to be very common today. They are now becoming one of the most popular options of income-generating works that can be done at one's convenience. They vary when it comes to the level of work. On-line data entry jobs are among the best internet posts to earn money online without investment.

You therefore have to be committed to the jobs so it is possible to satisfy the deadlines and quality levels demanded otherwise you might end up ruining a great working prospect. There are two kinds of information entry jobs. Data entry jobs may sound easy, but it's actually a daunting and compelling endeavor, and one needs to be competitive since there are many job seekers online who might have more experience. It's quiet easy to begin a data entry job. Data entry jobs in Delhi can be located through various on-line job portals.

As a beginner you ought to be patient enough to do the work first well before asking a huge pay. There are various kinds of Data Entry jobs to pick from. The majority of the data entry jobs are part time and offer a great earning to the workers. An additional way is the on-line data entry jobs.

You're able to make an application for jobs after completing the site's internet application. The great thing about such a part-time job is the abilities and knowledge you acquire there. Part time jobs for students are almost always available there and they are ideal for women and men.

Ever since your occupation is data encoding, you should buy a computer that's competitive enough to manage the processing. When it's for an internet job an offline job. Especially, in case you have taken up online jobs then you have to possess excellent typing skills as you're paid on the grounds of words per minute. On-line data entry jobs are becoming increasingly more abundant due to the net.

There are many sorts of information entry jobs to pick from. They encompass a wide variety of various needs. If it comes to internet marketing jobs, online data entry jobs are among the outstanding jobs that folks are doing.

10   KINDLE DIRECT PUBLISHING

It's possible for you to select a plan for every one of your books. Easily portable Yet another advantage of publishing eBooks is that they're effortlessly portable when compared with paper printed books. The more stuff, the more cash you've got the capability to make. If you've got another Micro SD card on hand, consider inserting that into your device and see whether it works. If still, the Micro SD card is not functioning, we ought to make sure in the event the card itself isn't the issue.

Probably not cost effective for the extra $ Internet delivers superb, cost-free marketing and advertising possibilities. Email marketing has become the most effective kind of marketing. It's simple to get confused about what's important if building your company. Make certain you are permitted to run a business from your residence. Social networking is one of the list of methods to acquire better at. Email Lists Are Inexpensive. The technology that allows you to set up auto series is affordable, you can begin in some instances free and work your way up to a greater account.

Normal 0 If you're searching for a great method to earn some passive income you should start looking into Kindle digital publishing. Kindle digital publishing is a rather very good means to develop into a published author and produce a lot of money. Kindle self publishing has offered e-book writers brand new possibilities to make money. Line editing might be done together with the proofreading.

Some of the absolute most effective Amazon ebook writers produce a a little fortune through the job they do. Other authors aren't your competitors. If you've got a contributing author make certain that you include them. If your book is non fiction, it's also recommended to include pertinent biographical details. Not that you asked how to promote your book. Someone who reads one particular book will probably read another book in precisely the same niche, therefore it is helpful to be paired in the readers' minds. Pick the second choice if you are publishing a public domain book.

Developmental editing with somebody who's genuinely interested in your book. If your book is fantastic, well, that's not sufficient to reach a wide audience, but it's a good beginning. It is possible to set your book as a portion of a series when it's being published. Say, you're trying to purchase a book about investing. You are able to enroll a single book, your entire catalog or anything between. Once the eBook is made on your own, or by a specialist, you may sell or circulate a great deal of copies. To earn money with Kindle self publishing, you will first must set a top quality eBook together.

You will require a great idea as well as a bright marketing and advertising program. It is possible to depend on several easy suggestions to raise the popularity of your publications and also to enhance income.

As always the actual answer lies somewhere in the center. If the issue is proven to be in the device, then attempt updating the device to be certain it is running the newest software. If nothing works out for you, there may be an issue with the device hardware and if that's the case, it is wise to find expert assistance. The one thing I care is whether

the book would fix my problems. Kindle accessing problem isn't a huge issue if you don't know the right approach to utilize your device. There could be some problems with the card formatting which may be causing the matter.

Once more, you'll need to consult local authorities to learn what licenses and permits you demand. Basically, you must stay within the limits of responsible legal and company behavior generally speaking. Thus, it's important to select your account carefully and register your device to prevent kindle signing in issues. It's very easy to make an account on Amazon, which hardly requires a number of minutes to achieve that. Therefore, if you're a Kindle user and searching for some advice to address your device's issues, then you don't need to be worried. In the event you face more problems or the device has problems, you can get in touch with Amazon customer care and they ought to have the ability to address your problem. The simplest method is to download Amazon's Previewer application that's a software edition of a Kindle.

11 EMAIL MARKETING

Email marketing makes it very simple for you to customize content so that you address your contacts by their names in order that they feel engaged and like you are speaking to them directly. Email marketing is getting to be one of the finest effective and affordable tools for internet marketing. Email marketing is an essential advertising tool for all businesses. There are many sorts of email marketing leads. Mass email marketing is a kind of email marketing that includes sending large quantities e-mail utilizing a tremendous list. Therefore, it is one of the most cost effective ways to get traffic and highly profitable. Mass e-mail marketing is extremely cheap in comparison to other advertising media and has proven over time among the absolute most helpful way of advertising.

If you haven't already, among the very first things you ought to do is to generate valuable email lists of your customers. Good email lists aren't easy to find. At length, you might look at renting email lists from marketing businesses.

To start with you want to make sure your emails aren't in jeopardy to wind up in your subscribers spam folder at their email services. Certainly, email isn't dead, but it's getting harder to do well. When an email is rejected, we will unsubscribe you. You may possibly possess the very best email ever written, but if your subject line doesn't catch the eye of the reader, it won't even get opened.

In case the email is from a reliable source and contains information applicable to their way of life, they might very well read and answer the messages. The email is going to have an increased visibility than a Facebook post. It's possible to schedule and automate your emails with the assistance of autoresponders. The email begins with the subject line. Every emails sent to a prospective customers can be regarded as as email advertising.

A well designed application along with exceptional marketing and advertising concepts will surely make your cell marketing a prosperous campaign. Make sure that you have good email advertising computer software. An outstanding email advertising campaign software is going to have the ability to compile a list of your very best email subject lines, in addition to your very best email ad copy that produced the most visitors. The email promoting software necessary for a karate school's email advertising campaign is inexpensive to buy and simple to install and manage. Must Track Visitors Good email advertising campaign software will measure not merely the email open pace, but also track the quantity of visitors that click on your link in your email in order to see your recommended website. If you've been using any other email advertising tool which you've found helpful, we'd really like to hear about doing it.

Email marketing is still among the most cost effective kinds of advertising on the net, but it has to be permission based or opt-in email advertising. Email marketing is just one of the most useful and cost-effective tools to promote your products and solutions. Email marketing is just the use of emails to promote your goods. There are many explanations as to why you should use email marketing to promote your business. If you're serious about email marketing, and it's a tested sales channel for your company, there are some essential metrics you should monitor (but not until you get a mature email advertising process). Bulk email marketing is recognized among the very best performing and yet affordable method to communicate information to existing and new customers to your company today.

Email marketing has a couple of advantages you won't find to any of the traditional advertising and marketing tools. Email marketing is just one of the best ways for a company to promote themselves and increase sales. however, it has to be carried out right in order to work. In case the bulk email marketing is done well, it can't only maximize visitors to your site, but in addition maximize your sales. Mass email marketing or bulk e-mail marketing is among the most cost effective techniques to acquire your message to your intended audience.

What to look for when picking an email marketing support. A superb email advertising service ought to have quite a few characteristics that permits you to tweak things so that you can receive the most bang for your advertising buck. When a customer is extended a distinctive privilege they respond well. Email marketing services is a significant part of our lives. SMS advertising services in UAE region is extremely low-cost!

38

12   HOW TO BECOME AN AMAZON ASSOCIATE

You are then going to be requested to add your site details. Producing something worthwhile is far more successful, and you receive the attention and respect of expected customers that manner. Possessing the ability to get ads on your pages with your content is excellent. Whether it's a small business seeking to benefit from the Amazon affiliate program or individual Amazon associates, there are lots of opportunities to create revenue. There's no need to purchase and keep stock. Among the strategies to produce money on HubPages is to utilize Amazon Capsules in your Hubs.

Ending with a Top 3 comparison chart is among the most effective things that you can do.

On-line success today is about long-term thinking. In the same way, you are going to find that you've got much more success if you're making useful and intriguing posts and should you turn into a regular on the website. You can see that success with affiliate marketing is really straightforward.

The next thing to do is to have a look at the backlink profile for the page. When you register for hosting they'll send you an email which offers you accessibility to cPanel, together with your login credentials. The automated call will request that you confirm the pin number. When you put in your telephone number, a pin number appears on the monitor. Indicator number two might be the backlink profile. Since you can see we finally have quite a few keywords we can investigate to find the competition level of each item. There are a lot of WordPress plugins that will benefit your website in a variety of ways.

Based on your specialty, you can select unique forms of links. The next thing to do is to get links, banners, or widgets for your website. Fortunately, you don't require that many for your website to function properly. Before you jump into building your website, you're likely to have to choose a niche to target. The very best part, however, is that HubPages is also part social-networking website, so simply by being on HubPages you will start to draw traffic interested in your topic and searching for recommendations. It's simple for your site to become bogged down and perform much slower once you are in possession of a massive site with a whole lot of content and media. The steps above gave you all you want to know to begin creating your own site.

When it has to do with making money online you're likely to have a great deal of options available. You may still make good income by promoting cheaper products in the event the volume is high enough.

Frankly, it can be very overwhelming just choosing a web business type to run with. If you're interested in developing a long-term business you'll inevitably will need to compile a site. As stated above in affiliate marketing you're able to promote many varieties of things. What's Affiliate advertising Affiliate Marketing is basically a profit-sharing business arrangement between a site operator, referred to as an affiliate, and an internet business, called the vendor or merchant. If you are a newcomer to Affiliate

Marketing, you will undoubtedly be experiencing information overload, as you attempt to create sense of the huge minefield of information which is the world of Affiliate Marketing. It is possible to become an affiliate for virtually any business so long as they've got an affiliate program in place.

13 BULK SMS TEXT MARKETING

BULK SMS MOBILE MARKETING

Traffic is the life blood of every online business. You need fresh, targeted traffic for your business to grow. Bulk Sms Advertisements put your business right in front of a captive audience. With it indeed your business is showcased right on the screen of the cell phone of potential clients. Traffic means profit and the more targeted, relevant traffic you have, the more money you will make.

With Bulk SMS text marketing you can reach almost anyone with a cell phone, including a smart phone. It mostly brings the better results than expected. Earlier, most people thought that SMS mobile marketing is merely too promising for comfort. If you genuinely want to make mobile SMS marketing effective not only as a campaign but effectively utilize it to promote your business, then you need to learn more tips about how you could exploit its features to completely enjoy it. With SMS mobile marketing you get to pick the people you would like to send the message to because you wish to supply them the products which you sell or the services which you offer. It is possible for you to draft your private message to guarantee precision. It is crucial to steer clear of spam messages. If however you get a text message on your phone, you will normally have to open it before you can even consider deleting it, therefore it really is logical to read it first. The text has to be plain and no additional work for the text is required. The most significant thing you have to do is to compose the text and join it with the URL of your site.

Text marketing services are turning into a developing platform for business promotions. When it has to do with text advertising solutions, they promote an all in one marketing service in the place where they combine several services at one time. A text service ought to be able to send messages quickly. An excellent text service needs to be in a position to deliver text messages in a rapid and timely method. It is very important to work with text messaging service which understands the business's needs.

Basically, mobile promotion is a simple context-based marketing that's really very specialized. It is simply the process of conducting marketing and advertising activities tapping on the cell phone as a delivery channel. In order for it to be effective, it must be incorporated into any businesses' general marketing strategy and accompanied by e-mail marketing as well as other forms of advertising. It enables measurable results which is one of the most critical requirements of any marketing project.

It is possible to also incorporate SMS Text Marketing to your site, permitting you to contact new clients. As mobile marketing presents new and advanced advertising and delivery alternatives, there is need to master them well as a way to execute the procedure well and achieve the desired effects. There are lots of people around who do not understand how powerful mobile text marketing is.

You put money into bulk SMS software as it is an affordable tool to create communications messages to a huge volume of individuals at exactly the same moment. Bulk SMS software also

features a choice to greet your customer by making use of their names and surnames. Your cellular text program is permission-based, and therefore you need to make sure that you give your customers a great reason to opt-in and get your deals. If you are a business owner wanting to develop your advertising program, then text message marketing can address your problem.

Benefits of Text Marketing service

There are several advantages of SMS service to local businesses when using texting service for marketing their goods or services. Another substantial benefit of text message advertising solutions, are they can be put into place in minutes and results can be understood in the very first day (depending upon your text message advertising solution chosen).

Text message marketing is a method of reaching customers throughout the medium of SMS. Second, it is the only marketing campaign that you can engage in that will not require you to spend so much. Employing text marketing as your advertising strategy is the best solution for virtually any company. So adding a quick code for HELP where it's possible to call back and clarify would be an additional good point to ensure in your campaigns. Well, it is only vital in a text promoting campaign that you've got the mobile numbers of all of the right people who will benefit from the merchandise or services you provide. Whenever you have your cellular marketing and advertising campaign designed you should make sure certain things are covered though. Given the appropriate conditions, you truly can run a prosperous SMS advertising campaign for literally pennies per message.

14 DEVELOPING MOBILE APPLICATIONS

The majority of the enterprise applications contain large quantity of data which belongs to the information of the business. In the present business environment, mobile applications are essential to create a positive effect among your possible clients. It can help in easy communication and retaining them consistently. Build Brand A mobile application enables you to customize the image of your organization in a manner that you find fit. Developing mobile applications is a topic that you need to understand if you are a company in the present society. Mobile web applications also tend to decrease the printing costs your business has to devote annually.

Due to its isomorphic nature, the framework assists in SEO in addition to loading the pages quickly. With that said there are tons of different frameworks out there which permit you to use your skills to construct a cell app. Firstly the framework simply didn't need to work properly. For developers in addition to the app owners, Laravel framework provides numerous features and advantages.

Instant application saves not just a lot of storage space in the mobile, but likewise the user's time. Developing native applications for all of the app growth platforms is still viewed as a challenge as it is extremely costly and time-consuming. On-line web applications are able to take care of tasks that range from small to mass-market tasks and can increase the total productivity and reach of your organization in ways which were not always possible. They have been shown to reduce the time and expenses of using customer service resources to explain various aspects of your business.

The majority of the companies providing mobile app development in Houston can be reached through their sites. Without any second thoughts, every company or a brand ought to have a mobile app that may create revenue for the company and convert leads. Very few businesses have mobile apps of their very own. Any business that is just beginning in the industry ought to take the aid of an app development vendor who is experienced in the related field. Many companies believe building and developing app is a costly procedure but before developing it if a specific prototype is maintained then it isn't in any way difficult. If you're a mobile application development company, an individual have to bear in mind that mobile development costs are connected to the quantity of platforms the enterprise makes the decision to support which also comprises the skills necessary for mobile app development.

If you wish to test app on iPhone simulator, and you are looking for the app that enables you to target the competitive market, then mobile app growth services in

Hyderabad are the perfect option to get, install and use for your company brands. As a developer, you will be thrilled to utilize it for the internet app and API development.

A quick idea to get precisely what you are trying to find is to take into consideration the apps you would really like to work on and check their cellular app development team. It is simpler to use mobile apps. Most individuals may be surprised to learn that mobile apps have been part of phones for at least twenty decades. A cell app is created while

the database integration occurs. To comprehend the length of time it takes to construct a cell app, let us take a closer look at the manufacturing procedure and other project factors from beginning to end.

An app ought to be dynamic and robust. Also, a cell app is more feasible to deal with and be used than a site. Even past the experience, mobile apps are wonderful for keeping brand recognition high. Once your cellular app is prepared for launch, you may choose the most suitable category in which you need to include your application. Possessing a mobile app for your company is an apt strategy for you too.

15 SOCIAL MEDIA MARKETING

Social networking is a phenomenon that you will need to master if you need your business to excel. It is possible to use social media to gather a great deal of information about your customers and prospects and you may also use it in order to look after customer relations. Social networking is a networking device that is extremely efficient and dependable for people and groups alike.

Today, nearly everybody is using social media sites.

SEO marketing providers can choose the correct set of keywords and make your company website rank higher in the various search engines. The majority of the search engine optimisation marketing businesses offer custom and tailor-made solutions to coincide with one's requirements.

External promotion is an immediate reflection of how successful you are going to be.

If your company is not the top selection, then it means your company is lacking something which other businesses already have a lead on. When you post about your organization and products on a blog, you're increasing your on-line presence. Since not all businesses could afford to employ a social networking manager, you ought to figure out first the particular platform that gives out the best outcomes. You ought to make sure your Page reflects your present company and direction. Among the most common social advertising goals is to enhance communication. You should clarify the exact same to make sure that the marketing efforts can be tracked on a normal basis. You must find a way to create social media work for you!

Once more, it is a simple and efficient marketing strategy. It is built around the concept of creating free content to build an audience.

Email marketing is easily the most cost-effective kind of digital marketing. It is all about relationships as well as interactions and influences. It enables you to reach potential customers and stay ahead of your competitors.

16   FACEBOOK MARKETING

Facebook is the largest social media platform online. As is true with giant software platforms, Facebook is perpetually changing. Along with regular videos and client. Videos, it provides the live and 360-degree choices.

Facebook offers one an opportunity to use informal chat to publicize one's item, goods or services. Facebook is a platform to get exposure for a Realtor. When used in the appropriate fashion, Facebook can be a superb resource for connecting communities of family and friends and opening a worldwide field of communication.

Facebook is a confluence of several people. It has a number of other social features like groups, events, and tagging, which makes it possible for people to rapidly connect with one another by taking full benefit of the ability of Facebook as an advertising solution. Facebook isn't a new medium anymore. It is an excellent place to provide incentives and a perfect place to interact with customers.

Over the last few decades, Facebook marketing has come to be an important part of many a little business' plan of succeeding. It has become an excellent tool for getting one's content in front of millions of web surfers and for driving traffic to a website. Pinterest marketing offers the chance to take pin boards and pins across to all the men and women you need to. Whoever has ever read anything on digital marketing understands the genius of Gary. Perhaps you noticed that many of the tips people use in email marketing to cut back complaints and confusion are the very same in chat. Fan Page marketing can be extremely effective, but only as long as you're ready to catch the customer's eye long enough to make her or him stay on your page to find out what your service or product is about.

A great deal of men and women approach Facebook marketing as a significant job. Facebook marketing is not magic, it is a testing game. For a small business success, Facebook relationship marketing is extremely potential.

It is something that every entrepreneur must have spent time to master its application.

Profiting from Facebook isn't a secret anymore, and among the most talked about ways to earn money.

Making your profile personal and with a great deal of relevant information can truly boost your likelihood of getting people to find you. You should make sure you give your visitors every possible opportunity to have view of your posted message.

Therefore there's also a big chance to earn money beyond geographical limits utilizing the social networking platforms. You have got to wait and put in your efforts for some opportunity to earn money. Using Facebook, preparing a campaign is really easy to accomplish.

Facebook marketing can be complicated and much less simple as it would seem. It is the most untapped trend in Internet marketing right now. Don't forget your primary goal that's to market your organization. Affiliate marketing consistently provides a great chance of making money from social networking networks.

When it has to do with indexing things on the web, Google prefers original content. Social media is growing ever more popular, among the most famous being Facebook.

Select the sort of official Facebook page you want to create. Most important of all you have to construct your own Facebook page which ought to give information on the niche you're interested in. Facebook fan pages are another popular means to try to attract a purchasing audience.

Without knowledge of the way to use Search Engine Optimisation people won't be driven to your site. Purchasing a web site is the initial stage of a practice.

To earn money here you need to have a site or a blog. Developing a site is easy. Having your own site or blog does improve your odds of getting approved by Google.

You could also make a page for your organization.

Believe it or not Facebook isn't just somewhere to meet friends, it's also an excellent place to create some extra cash. Facebook isn't a wildly popular spot for making money on the internet. Since Facebook is quite a restricted in all you must delete your pending requests. Applications Facebook also has applications which could be games or various tools that are incorporated into Facebook.

Facebook is now an addiction for millions of individuals. It's also different than how most individuals will say to advertise by using Facebook. Recently, the social networking site Facebook has gotten many more popular and has come to be a most important source of traffic.

Which means in the event that you help your friends to earn money, then you're helping your earnings to grow. The more you teach your friends how to make money from Facebook, you'll also earn more money. The more you bring friends on this website the more you are able to earn money. Put simply, attempt to add as many friends as you're able to. You are able to find out what people are speaking about, what's trending, and catch up with family and friends on a normal basis.

Profiting from Facebook isn't a secret anymore, and among the most talked about ways to earn money.

Making your profile personal and with a great deal of relevant information can truly boost your likelihood of getting people to find you. You should make certain you give your visitors every potential opportunity to acquire on board. Therefore there's also a big chance to earn money beyond geographical limits utilizing the social networking platforms. You've got to wait and put in your efforts for some opportunity to earn money. Using Facebook, preparing a campaign is really easy to accomplish.

 Social media is growing ever more popular, among the most famous being Facebook.

It can be complicated and much less simple as it would seem to be, yet, it is the most untapped trend in Internet marketing right now.

17 PARTICIPATION IN USABILITY TESTING OF APPS

Apps have to be adapted accordingly. An app constructed for 58 year adult differs from an app made for banking professionals. For instance, if you need your app to be employed by iPhone users, you are going to be working in Objective-C or Swift, and your merchandise is going to be sold in Apple's App Store.

Usage with Other Apps

When the app under test is operating in parallel with different apps, there ought to be no interference. There are a number of reasons why users uninstall apps. On the reverse side are apps with a high price tag targeting a very particular set of users.

Network Speed

The app should be checked on a selection of networks with variable speed. At this point you are looking for new photo filter apps.

In a lot of the circumstances, there is a better approach to welcome your users. As a great bonus, additionally, it provides enough visual clues to figure out, the way the user could end up there, and what are the available alternatives to get out. Users enjoyed the part of not having to experience additional actions. Users of Android devices won't be in a position to utilize your app. The functionality and performance of the app are tested regularly together with improvement. Usability depends upon target audience.

A great deal of tools are offered in market to understand user behaviors. Particular tools are used to control the implementation of evaluations to additional review the real results against the anticipated advantages. Naturally there are different tools than Fitnesse. Testing has ever been a crucial part of creating high excellent computer software.

The XCTest framework permits us to run performance test together with our unit or UI tests. XCTest frameworks can measure the operation of the block of code within the unit or UI tests.

Quality assurance and operational blindness

In addition to usability testing, the growth of cellular apps has an important part in the coverage of the various terminals. Regardless of the advantages that medical mobile app development can provide every stakeholder involved with the sector, there are a number of concerns to consider before going into the market.

Part of designing great user experiences is to lower complexity and boost usability. After taking the course you'll possess a highly effective comprehension of UX and the critical activities associated with the area. Pairing With shortening shipping cycles, there's a larger demand for integration of several distinct elements of an element improvement.

Client participation is highly advised. In addition, the participant doesn't interact with a moderator.

A well-designed product is not just simpler to use. Having sympathy with the user's goals is essential to building a product they'll love. Of course you've got, and so will your customers if your site or product isn't user-friendly.

Usability testing is part of Non-Functional Testing. It does not have to be expensive or time-consuming. The handbook testing is still dominating the testing marketplace. Testers will begin the testing from user registration page end to finish. The tester can record and play several measures that are expected to perform testing. The testers aren't knowledgeable about the undertaking and are approaching the issue openly. Of course not every tester will have accessibility to each conceivable phone and tablet.

With the appropriate automation framework, you can control what it requires to compose a test. Since tests run in their very own procedure, we know they must synchronize. If your tests are breaking, then have a look and see the reason why they are breaking. Running user tests are fantastic for improved understanding of your users and what's working in your goods.

18 REGISTERING ON REWARDS SITES

You can readily get stress-free by registering on our website. You might even realize that you prefer the cell site to the desktop website. For example a fantastic survey site would permit you to pay or receive money-using Pay pal. Yes, if you understand how to spot legitimate paid survey websites and prevent the scams.

Out of the desperation of getting an increasing number of coins at no cost, individuals come across a variety of websites that claim to get Robux online free of charge either through generators or a different manner. Such websites are not only helpful for individuals but also beneficial for companies to interact with one another. Among the finest and well-known websites to become relaxed is VentAllOut. Some complain that the site is a bit outdated. There are websites offering money only for registering in their website.

It is possible to win cash on the internet by simply registering and producing a free account in some specific sites. Online paid surveys are a simple way to make extra revenue online for Malaysians. In truth, it is among the simplest legit techniques to make money on the internet.

A different way to win a lot of money online is to just join on poker websites. Earning money during spare time through the web is the upcoming major thing.

You may either request cheque payments or have the funds electronically transferred. You can opt to get your payments via Paypal or Check. The customary payment for registering for business offers or filling out surveys is usually quite low, but they're informative when it regards their offers. Pick the features that you want to enhance your account. Your Virtual Account can't be redeemed for money. The Virtual Account is not a charge card. There are several more completion incentives listed on their website. Rewards vary depending on the survey kind and the company conducting the survey. Even should you not qualify, you will get an immediate reward of $5, once you join the panel. You will also receive Star Rewards accumulated dependent on the gifts purchased by means of your registering.

If you are lucky, sometimes you're able to come across a survey that pays up to $5 based on the length. Anyone who would like to be counted in the survey can go to the site and finish a quick checklist. Even though you may not obtain the highest-paying on-line survey offers, you may rest assured you are going to get paid for everything you earn.

You might get disqualified from a few of their surveys, however you will receive 15 point compensation for your efforts. Surveys are among the simplest approaches to win some money. Paid surveys also provide you the choice of totally free products. The greater end surveys run out surprisingly quickly so it is necessary to stay tuned and be watching out for their new offers.

19 **DOCUMENT TRANSLATION**

You can see that there are many steps included in translation. When it has to do with translation of documents, chances are that it may contain some classified and sensitive information in connection with the business. If something goes wrong in your translation, there's absolutely no doubt which you will be held responsible for the very error. Document translation is getting an important element of businesses all around the world. It ensures that every document you send to another country match up their country's standard rules and regulations. To put it simply, legal document translation is a difficult undertaking. So employing a professional document translation of a company is a great alternative.

Translation is far more than changing documents from one language to another. Translation Quotes based on time are certainly the safest option from the Translation services company viewpoint as it covers unforeseen translation issues like formatting. If you're skilled in medical translation, you can initiate the business with only yourself. The remedy to medical translations lays in the usage of medical translation specialists. An

internet translation may be a legitimate aid to linguistic decipherment. Finding an accurate translation is fairly simple to find. Ensure that you've an accurate and viable translation for your cell application.

Basically, to earn a translation certified, it has to be accredited based on the laws in the destination country. Mobile translation, because of the essence of the sort of display they'll require, must also be briefer in order in order to fit on the pages. Accordingly, picking a translator or translation company should be accomplished with the utmost care. It is very important to locate a translator with of knowledge and somebody who can ensure a good service.

The translation wasn't about language difficulties but something that trickled into lots of new seams of a communication strategy for a business searching for new horizons. There's a whole lot more to translation than you may think. Technical manual translation is only one of the services you are able to avail in internet localization businesses. In order to get a complimentary immediate quote you have to pick languages and upload the documents. Possessing an accurate translation of the assignment can be quite valuable to students striving to learn a new language. It can be a slow process because it is not an automated process.

Some document translation businesses provide 24-hour or 72-hour turnaround times for smaller projects, while others are going to vary from 5 business days to a few weeks in length. Virtually all document translation companies post their confidentiality policy on their site or in their advertising and marketing materials, and that means you can be sure your documents will be safe and secure. Assuring you of high excellent translation support, document translation companies employ people from various nationalities that are natives to the 50 unique languages that the provider has the ability to translate your documents into. Many document translation companies offer customer support services 24 hours every day, seven days weekly, which means you can easily monitor the status of your project and have any questions answered easily. They offer online submission options, which means you don't have to worry about packing and shipping your

documents and waiting to receive a confirmation of receipt. They offer an instant quote online, which can make it easier to manage your budget.

A language translation service is currently a prerequisite when it has to do with global communications and marketing. Proficient translation services can be useful in many locations. By making use of a translation agency you can be assured you will get top high quality translation services.

Not all translation businesses can pass your standards and not one of them has the exact same capability and features. Now it is likewise important to put money into a translation company that meets your standards. Professional translation businesses provide a wide scope of services for businesses and people who need reports, brochures, letters and manuals translated into another language. They offer a number of services for companies and individuals who need high quality documents.

Picking the most suitable translation professional company from several ones can be critical.

There are some excellent Translation Services in Hyderabad. It is possible to also employ a professional translation service provider to have your job done. Engaging the help of a translation agency is completely critical in ensuring your company remains successful in the tough environment of global enterprise. While there are numerous folks who provide translation solutions, just a few specialized firms can offer medical translation. Of course there are many Spanish translation services online from individual freelancers to huge businesses.

20 JOINING SURVEY PANELS

If you aren't from the United States, you will still able to find survey panels you may join but you might not have as many survey opportunities as someone from the US. There are an infinite number of survey panels out there which you are able to join, and all of them claim to be the very best.

To make it simpler for you, we've listed down the things that legit companies aren't going to do so you are able to rate the site simpler. By collecting information from the targeted group of people, the organization will tailor and boost their goods or services to raise their company profit. After all, all businesses wish to boost their product sales in the industry. In some instances, customers could contact customer support, and they could receive their money.

Give a try and you're going to observe how members are enjoying the benefits of being a true member. One benefit of Survey Junkie is the fact that it is quite easy to use and you will be able to secure the points awarded instantly. For completing profile, you do not just become eligible for more opportunities but also get rewarded in the form of rewarding points. On iPoll dashboard, you'll be in a position to check what survey opportunities are readily available to you.

If you are interested in making passive on-line income, you shouldn't ever look at joining survey panels only. Earning money is just one of the things which everyone is after for. Joining survey panels are ideal for stay at home parents who wish to earn some excess money.

My preferred means of making money on the internet is affiliate advertising. After all, it is affiliate marketing.

The site was made so as to permit consumers to share their opinions online. Even in the event you don't have any experience with survey websites or are not technology savvy, you may produce a profile and begin in a few minutes. It's better to sign up for at least one survey site, as you usually won't make a lot at the same site. If you have decided you wish to join a paid survey site or two, you simply ought to make sure that you research the sites first to make certain they are a legit paid surveys site. When you log onto their website, the design is clean and easy. Scam sites will lack a whole lot of important details. Some sites reward cash for each and every survey they finish. There are a lot of legit survey sites out there which is easy to use.

If you are not invited on every survey that does mean that you are disqualified. Paid survey is a chance for business brands to get the actual feedback from the general public. A paid survey is just a survey that you may take and make a reward for doing this.

Getting started taking online surveys

There are a few very important things to keep in mind if you opt to take paid surveys. Each survey includes a TraitScore. Some surveys take a couple of days and a few take a couple of weeks. You get a minimum of one survey each day from PaidViewpoint, but a lot of them are low paying TraitScore surveys.

Most likely, you will get one survey per week. If you are lucky, you will get a few surveys every week, but that is not common. If you are not already acquainted with internet surveys then you have to read the how to make money by taking online surveys. Survey invite rate is dependent on your TraitScore. The greater your TraitScore the more income you can make per Biz Survey, which in general pays the absolute most.

Survey Junkie is a wholly legit means to make money. It is one of the oldest panels out there. Give a try and you're going to observe how our members are enjoying the advantages of being a true member.

When you log onto their website, the design is clean and easy. Scam sites will lack a whole lot of important details. Some sites reward cash for each and every survey they finish. There are a lot of legit survey sites out there which it is possible to use.

21 HOW TO EARN FROM HUBPAGES

Without traffic you can't make money from Hubpages. So, if you would like to generate some income from it, you've got to submit contents of value which would attract customers. There are a number of different techniques that are being used to earn money on HubPages and regardless of what your talents are, you can use one to make money here.

Another means is to commit your own money to it. In the event you hadn't guessed already, earnings for the typical person who only submits a couple of parts of content are next to nothing. Passive income is the best type of revenue. The advantages are that they're shared on social websites. The second benefit is that it is possible to make a lot of sales within the niche (particularly when it is the type of content that most people love).

It is true, you can earn money at HubPages by referring new individuals to join the site! Before you can find out the way to earn money, you need to understand the method by which the monetization procedure works on HubPages. The manner that you may make money is via the affiliate links that show up on the pages. If you would like to make significant money, you will need to choose your topics according to what people are searching.

Join with hubpages now and you may be earning money within a couple of days. You can earn money without so much as writing a hub. If you're looking to earn money on HubPages and I'm talking dollars, not cents following is a fast and simple guide. If you wish to earn full-time money you're going to get to work and work hard. The best method to earn decent money is to write about things that lots of individuals are looking for.

Everybody is welcome to submit an application for the Apprenticeship Program. In each instance, when you register for a program through HubPages, you're provided an exceptional affiliate ID. You've got to register for the HubPages Earnings Program so as to access the rest.

Writing online does earn an excellent part-time income for many writers, but you have to adhere to it. There are a number of ways to make money on the internet at no cost and the one that I have lately discovered is writing for hubpages. Don't forget, it is FREE to join, so you don't have anything to lose.

A lot of people are making a living through writing articles and you'll discover that once you get started earning just a little bit of cash, it is going to become addictive and you'll actively start trying to find methods to secure better at producing money making hubs. Not every one of the articles in your account is going to be edited at exactly the same time, but you can have more than 1 article selected over time. Some articles take me a few hours to write, others might take up to five hours to write. All 3 methods might also be employed to virally advertise your articles. If you believe you can write a few articles and earn a fortune, again, that isn't true. Actually, as soon as you have written many

articles with good content, you might realize that while you're sleeping you are in fact earning money with Adsense.

If you visit the help pages you will find all of the info you have to have in order to acquire your very first article put together and published. When you run an affiliate site, you must stick to a single niche and mine out every potentially valuable keyword it is possible to find. You can also run a website such as Sweetbearies Art Workshop. Men and women go to the website, read the written content or purchase an item and leave the site. Content sites are a great way to enhance your income, but most of your money is going to be earned from your own sites.

Write as much content as possible about as many valuable keywords as possible. Individuals who get approved for AdSense get qualified for several explanations. In order to earn money from the affiliates you must register with them individually. You might locate a high paying niche that doesn't have a good deal of competition and after that you may be in a position to do it.

22 REAL ESTATE INVESTMENT

Real estate is a tangible asset that could offer income you don't need to work for.

Everyone wants the actual estate they own to appreciate in value.

Realtors and brokers also have the capacity of creating money on account of the reports. The realtors act as information hub for people wanting to purchase property.

Each kind of investment has its very own associated risks and rewards.

Real estate investing for a career can be rewarding in addition to satisfying.

Well, only as long as you paid retail for your premises. While there are numerous things to put money into, property is still one of the most lucrative and the most volatile, sometimes. Most individuals want a property that is move-in ready.

Residential property typically represents the largest yield among its peers in the housing market. Residential properties located close to hospitals and schools is likewise an important consideration, particularly for residential homes fit for families.

The first thing you ought to know is the sort of property you're looking for. People will continue to get informed from every property. Learn to be an expert negotiator as you are ending a genuine property cope. If a rental property is totally occupied when you're buying it, you might not even consider vacancy prices.

The property should create a stable cash-flow. Make certain you inspect the property for needed repairs prior to making a buy.

If you don't understand how to look yourself, you aren't going to receive any properties. In case the property is something which you are selling, you need to make the repairs first. Your investment property also needs to be tax-effective and ought to provide superior depreciation allowances. It can be one of the most rewarding aspects of your financial portfolio.

If you wish to get properties, you ought to be talking to prospective sellers who would want to sell their assets quickly. To provide your property a boost in value, you may also enhance your premises by upgrading it. After you determine the property that you wish to get and the price tag you need to offer, it's time to assemble a letter of intent (an LOI) to submit to the present owner. Purchasing an investment property is one of the ways to continuously earn passive income and create your generational wealth.

23 DROPSHIPPING

Drop shipping is a rather lucrative business for everyone who would like to go into it. Although it has a lot of benefits and ease but it never means that it doesn't require your dedication. It is a very simple business to run. It requires a lot of thought before engaging into it

Because of the worldwide financial crisis, huge numbers of people have gotten jobless and bulk of them were hoping to engage on home-based business as an alternate chance of making money. There isn't any more satisfying means of earning than gaining a profit when staying at home. Think well of the sum of money you're going to make investments. Dropshipping is an excellent means to create big money fast, and about the perfect way to get rid of money, too. Trust is hardly earned that is the reason why you must preserve it as soon as you have gained it. It is essential in building a long and lasting relationship with your customers and your business partner.

Deciding on the correct domain name is the most important task as you wish to get a domain that's linked to your niche market and valuable for the on-line business. Inside my opinion it is simpler and safer to use a wholesale dropship list given by means of a directory but in the event you truly don't wish to pay a membership fee then it can be done, it will merely have a while. A directory have huge collection of wholesale dropshipping businesses. Utilizing a wholesale dropshipping directory To locate a dependable and affordable dropshippers for your company, you will need to use a reliable wholesale dropshipping directory. When you've narrowed your search to two or three wholesalers, order a range of each firm's products to get familiar with them. It is, obviously, essential that the directory website is well-monitored and maintained to eliminate any possible illegal or scamming businesses.

With careful research, excellent advertising strategies and ensuring your clients' satisfaction, your company will be prosperous. It is possible to extend your company internationally and mothers from throughout the world can order from you. Browse excellent sites online like SaleHoo who's ready to help you while you begin your own small business. The sum which you must invest so as to run a prosperous on-line company is not that high.

Locate a niche for the goods you desire to sell before ordering. If you've already decided on the kind of product you would like to sell then the upcoming crucial step is to find a dependable and trust-worthy wholesale dropshipping directory. Awful news too because others may have tried selling similar products with very little success. Yes, it really is possible even when you don't sell your own products and without needing to store anything in your backyard. One more thing you may try is contacting the manufacturer of the item directly since they may provide there own dropshipping support. The supplier is also accountable for fulfilling the orders and handling returns in some circumstances. That means you can locate your right supplier with the support of SaleHoo.

You need to know something about the business you wish to go into before handling a supplier. To make your company a success, you must advertise the merchandise you sell. Dropshipping businesses have become very popular and lots of people today are earning good incomes from their homes. Locate a supplier that you may use often in your dropshipping enterprise. All you have to think about is if you wish to expand your organization then invest a bit more of your capital. An eBay business by means of a dropshipper is ideal if you don't have money to get started with because you become paid before you must pay your dropshipper.

Usually whenever you're starting out your will need to pay your organization up front. It's possible to also access to local and global companies. In theory there's nothing to stop you finding your own businesses offering dropshipping services. however, it is riskier then utilizing a safe list that has been tried and tested and it's also more time consuming. So you will be sure to locate the companies that you want in a brief moment. Everything is accomplished by a dropshipper company for you.

Drop shipping is quite a lucrative business for everyone who would like to go into it. It requires a lot of thought before engaging into it. It is already in the market for several years now and if you are going to analyze its process, it is risky on the part of the retailers since it is your name that is being carried out not the drop shipper's name. Try to remember, retail price depends on the wholesale price and other overhead price. When setting up your auction you are going to have to make sure your reserve price is higher than the price which you need to pay the dropshipper.

You may make sales online using the keywords for both PPC and SEO. Without proper documentation, you are going to shed an eye on sales, and investments for example. On account of the development of woman and the very simple truth that their general love of new fashion that the sales of women's clothing isn't only an intelligent small business venture, but it's turning into a trend of its own. The shipper labels and ships everything and you only have to administer your auctions and pay a little fee.

The ability to be a thriving entrepreneur with drop shipping requires skills to create ads, drive visitors to a landing page and other advertising and marketing skills which aren't as challenging. A lot of individuals are inclined towards the benefits of dropshipping business because it has the liberty of setting the retail price, which isn't possible in internet affiliate marketing. One of the biggest benefits of dropshipping business are its high earning potentials It is not hard to begin working on immediately. Since dropshipping vs affiliate marketing has turned into a hot subject of debate, you have to know the benefits of dropshipping company and what are the challenges behind it. Therefore, if you're currently on the lookout for the the easy and quick method to success, you may not readily find it.. What's more, you ought to focus on the strategy we've put together. Essentially, it's a web-based purchase fulfillment strategy in which you accept the customer orders and the supplier entity will manage the hassles of product shipment for your benefit.

In my opinion it is simpler and safer to use a wholesale dropship list given by means of a directory but in the event that you truly don't need to pay a membership fee then it can be done, it will only have a while. Utilizing a wholesale dropshipping directory To locate a trustworthy and affordable dropshippers for your company, you want to use a reliable wholesale dropshipping directory. Whenever you have narrowed your search to two or three wholesalers, order an assortment of each corporation's products to get familiar with them.

Just as with any other business the caliber of customer service is the crucial element to maintaining one's business. You're always just one product away from your success, and thus don't stop trying. There are lots of high selling products readily available, some of them looks very appealing but you ought to be careful.

You would like to find Etsy sellers or any other ones that are willing and ready to actively communicate with you. You've got to keep in mind that Etsy sellers are amazingly passionate about their brands. Dropshipping is the ideal technique employed by wholesalers to draw in more potential sellers. Fortunately, a number of

Etsy sellers will be pleased to work with you and make it possible for you to resell their merchandise!

You need to know something about the business that you want to go into before managing a supplier. You've got to study the business, know your industry, constantly figure out ways to boost your company, understand what it is that your clients want, effectively deliver the things that they wish to them, have excellent customer support, and a whole lot more.

You don't need to cover the shipping of products to your customers. Drop shipping is a rather lucrative business for anybody who would like to go into it. It requires a lot of thought before engaging into it.

Everything is accomplished by a dropshipper company for you. So you will certainly locate the companies that you are seeking in a brief moment. You can also locate dropshipping companies which sell to you at wholesale rates. You are able to also access to local and global businesses. Logistics companies seek more efficiency.

To make your company a success, you must advertise the goods you sell. Browse sites online like SaleHoo who's prepared to help you while you begin your own business enterprise. An excellent online business is your own on-line gift store, already stocked with products or one which you design yourself.

With careful research, superior advertising practices and ensuring your clients' satisfaction, your company will be prosperous. Another great method to promote your business is getting your website optimized for SEO. Any legitimate business requires a great deal of hard work and dedication to be prosperous. Dropshipping businesses have become very popular and several men and women are earning good incomes from their homes. Locate a supplier you may use often in your

dropshipping enterprise. Dropshipping business gives many advantages of the on-line retailers. Further, if you're contemplating starting dropship business of supplements then the largest benefit is that you are able to be your own boss and work at home.

Because the time spent on your on-line business really depends on you. The more right selection of the item, the more are the odds of you being successful in your drop shipping enterprise. Another advantage of Tax ID is the fact that it is also not too pricey and is affordable for almost everyone.

Suppose you don't understand how to make money from your house, you can try dropshipping. The good thing about it is that you may begin earning money from your home fast. Think well of the amount of money you're going to make from the investments.

If you're saving on your purchases, you can see drop shippers since they are selling at a very low price. Whenever someone purchases something from your store, all you need to do is go over to the supplier and order the product which has been purchased and have it sent right to your customer in your company name. Sellers may also make their own websites. Dropshipping is the very best technique employed by wholesalers to entice more potential sellers.

Everything is accomplished by a dropshipper company for you. Although the business is a little family owned business, its program is entirely free. That means you will be sure to locate the companies that you are interested in in a brief time. It's possible to also access to local and global businesses. Starting any new company presents its own unusual challenges, however commercially minded or digitally

savvy you're. Let's explore a number of the very best international dropshipping companies it's possible to find.

You need to know something about the business that you want to go into before handling a supplier. To make your company a success, you must advertise the goods you sell. Browse great sites online like SaleHoo who's ready to help you when you begin your own business enterprise. You should also have to be aware on how things work in wholesale enterprise. Dropshipping businesses have become very popular and lots of folks are earning good incomes from their houses. Locate a supplier which you can use often in your dropshipping enterprise.

Every new dropshipping entrepreneur requires a powerful and coherent business strategy. One common mistake entrepreneurs make when starting a company is combining their personal and company finances. At times you can even receive a turnkey business to operate. When the customer is prepared to purchase the item, the original dealer will send the item right to the customer. There are many services out there which offer list of wholesalers that provide dropship services.

24. MAKING MONEY FROM MYSPACE ACCOUNT

MySpace is an excellent place to grab new organization. Whereas Myspace proved to be a two-dimensional link to the mostly silly portions of the net, Facebook would like to be your three-dimensional everything. Myspace is also the ideal selection for young, hip, techno savvy businesses, which want to use video, music and other kinds of content to boost their internet marketing efforts. Just having MySpace and a couple squalid videos on YouTube can never be the source of becoming famous.

Let's say you've got an account a hypothetical site. Therefore, the account was deleted rather than disabled. Now, there are a lot more stringent password requirements when you register for a new account anywhere over the world wide web. Instead of getting your payments reduced, by maintaining the identical payment, you're going to be saving yourself money. In times of low rates of interest, it might even be possible for you to boost your bond payments.

If your email address shows up where it shouldn't, you are going to be notified so it's possible to take action after possible. Am confident lots are fake or have several accounts but it is really famous which the on the internet networking principle is fast rising along with the selection of accounts growing by about 40,000 every weeks time. Before you begin making calls and sending out emails, you must make certain that you have an outstanding small business plan with realistic targets.

With a paid account you have to enter information regarding your on-line payment account so that it is going to integrate with the membership service (like Paypal or a normal merchant account). The thing is, the majority of the info given says you've got to be a search engine optimisation mastermind or a super affiliate using Adwords

as a way to earn money. If you own a website, it's quite easy to bring a PayPal donation button on your house page. Another very convenient means of earning money on the internet is via eBay. Currently you are able to choose from two distinct options online. All the information there's completely free, for instance, internet dating tips whom I send out each week via e-mail.

In teaches you a few of the marketing strategies that lots of super affiliates are using to earn a bundle with CPA advertising. Marketing a bookkeeping company can be done online and in person. Zero Friction Marketing is $77 and includes a 60-day money-back guarantee. It's possible for you to make business on ebay and can generate income fast. Fortunately, some businesses enable you to print out an emergency sheet access codes, permitting you to restore access to your account even in case you don't have your cell phone. If you're a small business proprietor, and you're considering Myspace as an advertising vehicle for your goods or services, you may want to think about your target demographic first. Password managers are a really good tool, but be sure you read the user guide and learn a couple of things about it when you dive in.

With just a little experience and patience you will encounter the most suitable items to earn money. The trick to generating money on data entry and digital assistant jobs is to make sure that you're on the ideal site and you're in a really legitimate job also. There are many methods using which the Teens can make money as they may sell their own items, totally free stuff on ebay, can begin an own ebay store etc.. To receive her attention ways to make her curious. Do not expect to earn a large amount of money at first, it takes a small time to become used to eBay. You're worried you may be doing the incorrect thing, wasting time and money on the incorrect platform.

In such sites, you can discover an individual anywhere in the united kingdom by looking for his name, postal code, contact number, place, job, school, interests, etc.. Likewise, your friends won't need to know about your most current projects at work in case you don't want them to. If you don't enjoy the notion of employing a password manager, you always have the option to utilize 2-FA instead. You may have a post about 8 strategies to earn money for a blogger one day and then how to advertise yourself the next and why I like cheese after that. Not every post will be gold. You don't need to get started with any particular TYPE of post or kind of content.

 Millions of individuals are still flopping to MySpace because it has the capacity of assisting you to keep in touch with your family and friends in any way times. You have two ways which you can immediately begin generating a fine income after you've obtained a great quantity of MySpace traffic which is Google AdSense or text ad traffic. Make money of MySpace You can also make money using your MySpace account in similar methods of earning from other social networking sites. The sum of money you get varies based on how many visitors and clicks received within that month. There are various ways to generate income from this social network website. There are a few simple tips on the best way to earn cash with MySpace that even the normal clients can utilize. The one I use is really one of the just one that allows unlimited myspace accounts for a 1 time fee that is very powerful.

Sooner or later, however, you're likely to need to cut it short. The point is that should not leave all the opportunities for somebody else to take. Having to cover a myspace tool for each myspace account you are likely to advertise with can be quite pricey and ultimately, not even well worth it.

Oftentimes, the break-up procedure is equally as difficult for the individual who's doing the breaking. Now in that brief period of time a few things happened. After all, if you're seeking your buddies, the ideal place to search for them and find them is on Facebook. It can be a bit complicated to skip a telephone call because I rarely have an opportunity to return calls during business hours, but it's what it is. Response has been quite good thus far. Nevertheless, you should make sure that you adhere to the rules of the article submission are else your articles may get declined.

Social public networking has become the best game filter in the progress of internet interacting. There are several free social networks on the internet that you could utilize to boost your organization up which would be literally hard to stay informed about all of them so select a handful instead. There are a lot of things online that are growing in popularity.

People today go there to have a list of absolutely free emails so that they can invite them. There isn't a way to add pages to a current lens, but you may add tons of content. Making a blog page is absolutely free, and you may make it about your on-line enterprise. When you have generated enough visitors for your site to read your love poems and quotes now you can earn money from your efforts. In case you've got a site of your own to give Google, it is possible to often submit your author profile as soon as you have at least five approved articles. You visit the website, search for the image you desire. There are a few other networking sites like Yuwie that don't have an issue with you advertising.

Once finished, you will be in a position to search certain keyword phrases to establish the groups that have alike interests to yours. There's no other niche out there that's so simple to penetrate and earn money like poetry because the demand for it's high which no one has yet been in a position to attain. Affiliate marketing

consistently provides an excellent chance of making money from social networking networks. Business is created around recommendation which causes a viral reaction around the world which is the reason so many businesses have come to be so famous today. There's a promising venture for earning money utilizing different popular social media websites on the internet.

If you opt to market on MySpace I highly suggest MyFriendBuilder. MySpace have implemented a blog network so that you can publish different post when you need and it doesn't cost you a dime to utilize it. Myspace is surely somewhere it's possible to make hundreds, or in case you do it right and spend a good deal of time, even thousands of dollars per day. Myspace is presently one of the largest social networks on the net and even on the planet. MySpace inspires a number of the worst.

You will receive a collection of totally free use pictures! You receive an array of images. Proceed to the image you need and click on it. Choose one particular theme or perhaps a couple and concentrate on getting enough excellent images to make it operate.

25 MAKING MONEY FROM EBAY

There are a variety of ways to generate income selling on eBay. Most individuals say that it requires money to earn money, not necessarily. There's a whole lot of money in the actual estate enterprise. Earn money online with eBay It is extremely simple to make money from eBay but you'll want to do a little bit of research and put in some effort here. With the development of internet, lots of people have already been earning money on the web. You're also likely to learn on how best to generate massive amounts of additional money monthly. In the future, buying products which sell for an important profit will earn you a ton more cash.

You need to make the most of your profits. Essentially, prior to buying a selection of products to sell on, you have to consider just how much profit you would like to make per item. Because of the financial downfall recently, individuals are concerned about income as their expenses continue to rise. If you wish to make significant income from eBay then you can eventually begin a store of your own, where you could add numerous items which can be bought by consumers. You don't take a massive investment since there are many loan programs that you may use that are there to assist you. You will constantly should survey the market to find out what products are selling and to think about the best places to source products for the highest degree of profit.

In case you haven't used eBay before I advise that you head over there and look it over. On figuring out how to sell on eBay, you discover that the very best thing to sell on eBay is a product that's been used, and is still in good shape. It's correct that eBay may be an exceptional approach to add to, or even to exceed, your present revenue stream but always keep in mind that there's no such thing as a get rich

quick scheme. Most people today start out with eBay among several part time working from home jobs, and start considering devoting more time to it once it will become successful. The very first thing you've got to learn about how to sell on eBay is to found your business on something which you love. After you learn to sell on eBay, you learn that it's essential for you to find out what's the very best thing to sell on eBay such that it attracts customers to purchase it. Consider working out how long you spend home-based on eBay, then examine the profit you earn.

For making money with eBay working from house, you ought to make sure you have listed your product with a terrific title, a nice and accurate product description, an excellent photo of your item and you must list your item at the proper price. You are able to also learn the way that it is possible to sell products on eBay, without a lot of investment. Examine the demand for the product prior to buying!

If you're looking for ways of creating money on the internet, you should consider eBay. There are lots of ways to create money online easily at no cost. So as to be successful with internet marketing, you will initially must learn the ideal methods to create money on the web. So, just stick to the hyperlink below and you are likely to discover the techniques to earn money online easily at no cost. Everywhere you look nowadays someone is attempting to learn how to earn money online from home.

Sell Stock Photography Photographers have an increasing number of alternatives when it comes to making money online. You will then have to concentrate on that specific method to generate money on the internet. If you're similar to me, and are searching for an easy, and more to the point, completely free means of discovering how to earn money online from home then you'll find Article Marketing right up your alley.

Promote Affiliate Products You don't require a site to market affiliate services and products. When it has to do with making money online, most men and women think that having a site of your own is critical. The site is extremely popular with internet shoppers. While setting up your own site or blog will be able to help you generate more sales, you can provide your services and earn a living online without a site. Whenever your blog is getting a high traffic, there'll be plenty of companies who wish to market on your blog to market their products to your visitors. So, you can begin writing on whatever you really feel like expressing in your blog or blogger's blog.

If you're looking for ways of creating money on the internet, you should consider eBay. There are a lot of ways to create money online easily at no cost. As a way to be successful with internet marketing, you will initially must learn the proper techniques to create money on the internet. So, just stick to the hyperlink below and you are likely to discover the techniques to earn money online easily free of charge.

The net has expanded market dimensions and complexity so that a good or service that wasn't previously profitable can be sold profitably on the web. It is a place that has a lot of opportunities to earn an income if you know where to find them. Fortunately, individuals are everywhere and the net has made it simpler than ever to get in touch with prospects. The internet provides the ideal platform for freelancers to make money by supplying services based on their skill sets.

For those who haven't used eBay before I suggest that you head over there and look it over. The very first thing you need to learn about how to sell on eBay is to found your business on something which you love. When you learn to sell on eBay, you learn that it's essential for you to find out what's the very best thing to sell on eBay such that it attracts customers to get it. Consider working out how long you spend home-based on eBay, then examine the profit you earn.

On figuring out how to sell on eBay, you discover that the very best thing to sell on eBay is a product which has been used, and is still in good shape. It's correct that eBay may be a fantastic means to add to, or even to exceed, your present revenue stream but always keep in mind that there's no such thing as a get rich quick scheme. Most individuals start out with eBay among several part time working from home jobs, and start contemplating devoting more time to it once it will become successful.

If you believe earning on the internet is a simple job if you believe it's a cakewalk you're incorrect! Making money on the internet can be fraught with avoidable pitfalls. If you're looking for ways of creating money on the internet, you should consider eBay. There are several ways to create money online easily free of charge. There are several to pick from to earn money on the internet. If you're seriously interested in earning money online, start a blog. You will then have to concentrate on that specific technique to generate money on the web.

You'll still need to have a web site, merchant account, sales funnel, lead magnet and several other items. The site Ebates catalogs almost them all. If you construct your own site, you'll have more control over the appearance and feel of your organization, but there are costs for web hosting services and monetizing your site in order to look at. There are also a number of websites where any normal joe can set a bit more than just chump change in their pockets.

The website is somewhat similar to Etsy and virtually anyone can earn money on the internet selling a range of items here. Before you promote your website, you need to have some considerable content there. The more information you've got on your website, the larger the traffic potential from the free search engines. Just building your Amazon affiliate site is one particular thing, but it's a totally different challenge

to get started bringing in the most suitable traffic that will convert into product sales as soon as they click through to Amazon.

26. MY RECOMMENDATIONS

MAKE MONEY HERE:

1. Make money promoting Article Forge. When telling your friends about Article Forge, use the following link: http://goo.gl/yTGf2M . Use the link to promote Article Forge to your subscribers, on your blog, forums, etc.
You'll earn 25% of their Article Forge subscription - including each time their subscription renews!

2. Create generational wealth with Trevo. Be our Life and Health Coach or Elite Customer by joining this Trillion Dollar Business.

Join here:

https://goo.gl/ub9PdE .

3. Referral Programs

i. This one is hot. Instantly earn 0.01 BTC for every one of your friends who joins Remitano.

Requirement: Your friend should trade a total of at least 2 BTC (both buying and selling counted). Commission will be credited directly to your account and can be used immediately. Sign up here and share your link:

https://remitano.com/btc/ng/?ref=danuds

ii. **Spin Rewriter.**

Spin Rewriter is the world's best article spinning tool. It works in a completely different way from everything else in the market. It actually understands the meaning of every single word and phrase, the meaning of your entire article, and it can spin it with a single click. It's pretty amazing.

You can give it a try at https://www.spinrewriter.com/?ref=2ab87.

Also, you can sign up as an Affiliate and earn 50% of every purchase of your referrals as commission and whenever they renew.

www.ingramcontent.com/pod-product-compliance
Lightning Source LLC
Chambersburg PA
CBHW080944170526
45158CB00008B/2363